Diseases and Disorders of Youth

Kids and Obesity

Gail Snyder

ReferencePoint
Press®

San Diego, CA

About the Author

Gail Snyder is a freelance writer and advertising copywriter who has written twenty-five books for young readers. She lives in Chalfont, Pennsylvania, with her husband, Hal Marcovitz.

© 2019 ReferencePoint Press, Inc.
Printed in the United States

For more information, contact:
ReferencePoint Press, Inc.
PO Box 27779
San Diego, CA 92198
www.ReferencePointPress.com

LIBRARY OF CONGRESS CATALOGING-IN-PUBLICATION DATA

Name: Snyder, Gail, author.
Title: Kids and Obesity/by Gail Snyder.
Description: San Diego, CA: ReferencePoint Press, Inc., 2019. | Series:
  Diseases and Disorders of Youth series | Audience: Grade 9 to 12. |
  Includes bibliographical references and index.
Identifiers: LCCN 2018017500 (print) | LCCN 2018017947 (ebook) | ISBN
  9781682824047 (eBook) | ISBN 9781682824030 (hardback)
Subjects: LCSH: Obesity in children—Juvenile literature. | Obesity in
  children—Treatment—Juvenile literature. | Obesity in
  children—Prevention—Juvenile literature. | Obesity in
  children—Miscellanea.
Classification: LCC RJ399.C6 (ebook) | LCC RJ399.C6 S64 2019 (print) | DDC
  618.92/398—dc23
LC record available at https://lccn.loc.gov/2018017500

Contents

A Global Crisis

Simon is fifteen and worried that he will not live to be thirty. The five-foot-eight (1.73 m) teen weighs 285 pounds (129 kg) and admits to having had a weight problem since he was ten. But what is different now, what has him so upset, is learning that he has some serious health problems. He is at risk for developing diabetes, a disease that leads to high levels of sugar in the blood. It is a potentially fatal condition.

He also has high blood pressure, a condition that over time could lead to heart failure or brain damage, and high cholesterol, which could lead to heart disease. Writing on a message board for obese teenagers, he says: "When I found out I was morbidly obese I wanted to change but I can't stop stuffing myself with junk food even though I know I'm killing myself. I don't know how to control myself."[1]

Concerned Groups

Although Simon's health problems used to be rare for teenagers, they have become increasingly common. That's because the number of young people classified as significantly overweight has increased tenfold in the past forty years. This dramatic increase troubles physicians, parents, researchers, national security officials, and others concerned about the welfare of young people.

One group that is especially concerned about the substantial weight many American children, teens, and adults are carrying is the American Medical Association (AMA), the country's largest association of physicians. In 2013 the professional group issued a statement declaring obesity a disease requiring treatment. Patrice Harris, a physician who sits on the group's board of directors, says, "Recognizing obesity as a disease will help change the way the medical community tackles this complex issue that affects approximately one in three Americans."[2]

> "When I found out I was morbidly obese I wanted to change but I can't stop stuffing myself with junk food even though I know I'm killing myself."[1]
>
> —Simon, fifteen years old and morbidly obese

Many parents are also paying closer attention to the state of their children's health. In a 2017 poll conducted by the University of Michigan, parents of young people under the age of nineteen were asked to identify which aspects of their children's health were causing them the most worry. Among their top concerns were lack of exercise and unhealthy eating, both of which can contribute to obesity.

Certainly, parents have reason to worry. A 2017 study reported in the *New England Journal of Medicine* predicted that by the time they reach the age of thirty-five, nearly 60 percent of today's children and teens are likely to be obese. The study found that the earlier a child's weight problem develops the greater the child's risk for adult obesity. For example, a child who is obese at age five has a nearly 90 percent risk of still being obese at thirty-five. Zachary Ward, a Harvard researcher who was the study's lead author, says, "Our findings highlight the importance of prevention efforts for all children as they grow up, and of providing early interventions for children with obesity to minimize their risk of serious illness in the future."[3]

Teens' Futures Are at Stake

Many experts predict that while it is true today's young people are heading for adulthood well overweight and out of shape, they also predict the number of years today's young people will spend as adults could be considerable fewer: obesity usually leads to early death. Jacob C. Warren and K. Bryant Smalley, directors of the Rural Health Research Institute at Georgia Southern University, in their book, *Always the Fat Kid*, frame the issue this way: "In order to truly change the current childhood obesity crisis, the weight of our children must be viewed as a real and present danger to their future. No less important to survival than clothing and shelter. But more importantly, it must be viewed as a modifiable danger—something that can be changed."[4]

"In order to truly change the current childhood obesity crisis, the weight of our children must be viewed as a real and present danger to their future."[4]

—Jacob C. Warren and K. Bryant Smalley, authors of *Always the Fat Kid*

In fact, according to the World Health Organization (WHO), a United Nations agency that focuses on public health, if the situation does not change, by 2022 there will be more obese children and adolescents in the world than underweight children and adolescents. At one time, children facing famine used to be a bigger world problem than children eating too much. Yet these two seemingly disparate populations have something in common: obesity is often linked to poverty, afflicting families who live in areas where fresh foods are neither plentiful nor affordable. The US Centers for Disease Control and Prevention (CDC), the government agency responsible for keeping Americans healthy, reports that young people who are Hispanic and Native American have higher rates of obesity than white people and African Americans.

In fact, obesity is already claiming the lives of many Americans. According to the news website Vox.com, obesity contributed to

Recent studies suggest that nearly 60 percent of today's children and teens are likely to be obese by the time they reach the age of thirty-five. Health experts say more attention is needed for this growing health problem.

the deaths of 4 million people in 2015. Science writer Julia Belluz writes: "This is a massive number: It's more than the deaths caused by traffic accidents . . . or other deadly issues that get a lot of airtime, like terrorism."[5]

Clearly, the obesity epidemic among young people is a serious issue that demands attention from physicians, parents, and government agencies if the trend is to be reversed. But young people often have a responsibility to learn good nutritional habits and to find ways to exercise. As Simon has already realized, if he does not change his ways, he may be looking at an early death.

Chapter 1

What Is Obesity?

Although the numbers of overweight people have grown substantially over the past forty years, being overweight was not always considered a negative. In fact, having some girth used to mean that one was well off. Says physician Carl J. Lavie, a cardiologist and obesity expert,

> We may think that obesity is a relatively new disease that emerged in the late twentieth-century, but it dates back to the prehistoric era. Twenty-five to thirty-five thousand years ago, the first [artistic] representations of the human body depicted obese females. At various times over the centuries, it has stood for wealth or stature, or even luck, in the case of plump Venus figurines used in primeval rituals. When it was deemed good and a sign of health, it typically signaled that someone was living a privileged life and didn't go hungry.[6]

Even the origin of the word has ties to the distant past. The word *obesity* comes from the Latin word *obesitas*, meaning "having eaten so much that one becomes fat."

But unlike most diseases, which often leave no outward clue as to their presence, what makes obesity different is that it cannot be hidden: children and teens who are significantly overweight have nowhere to hide. While the condition of youths diagnosed with other diseases might be known only by friends and family members, virtual strangers can quickly guess by the physical appearance of these children and teens that they are suffering from obesity. It can be painful to feel so exposed. One fifteen-year-old girl shared her frustrations on an online social network. Under the cloak of anonymity she writes:

> I feel like the elephant in the room all of the time, even though I know I am not the biggest person in my family, and I am hardly even the biggest person on the street or in our neighborhood. We live in Pennsylvania, which is the home of [Tastykakes] and the [Philadelphia] cheesesteak so that should tell you enough. I just hate being like this. I am 5'6" and I weigh 235 lbs. . . . I grew up constantly hearing things like "One of your legs could feed everyone in Africa," or "You're such a fat, ugly pig and I hate you."[7]

Body Mass Index

Yet even though people think they can tell who is obese and who is not, clinically determining whether a child or teenager is obese is not done by sight. Instead, determining whether someone is overweight or obese is accomplished using two easy-to-determine standard health measurements: height and weight. In the case of young people, their heights and weights are compared with others who are the same age, height, and gender. The comparison, called a body mass index, or BMI, is based on a formula. According to the formula, a person's weight is converted to kilograms and divided by their height in meters times two. The result can be looked up on a table gleaned from the weights of a large number of children and teens.

Moreover, the BMI can be expressed as a percentage for where the child or teen fits in with comparable peers. If that percentage is 95 or above—meaning that only 5 percent of children or teens of the same age and height weigh more than they do—the person is obese. If the percentage falls between 85 and 95, they are overweight. If the percentage is between 50 and 84, their weight is normal. If the percentage falls below 50 percent, they are underweight.

For example, according to a calculator on the CDC's website, a ten-year-old boy who is 4 feet, 6 inches tall (1.4 m) and

BMI is considered an accurate gauge of obesity. However, a person who has well-developed muscles could very likely have a higher BMI than someone who does not because muscle tissue is heavier than fatty tissue.

weighs 102 pounds (46 kg) is obese. Another ten-year-old boy of the same height who weighs 83 pounds (37.6 kg) is considered overweight. By comparison, a same-height boy who weighs 70 pounds (31.7 kg) is considered to be at a healthy weight.

The BMI was first used to determine whether people were obese or underweight nearly two centuries ago—it was developed by Belgian statistician Adolphe Quetelet. Since then, many scientists and physicians have come to accept BMI as an accurate gauge of obesity. The US Department of Health and Human Services (HHS), the federal agency responsible for monitoring the health of Americans, regards BMI as a useful tool. However, not all physicians agree.

BMI Limitations

Margaret Ashwell, former science director of the British Nutrition Foundation, a food and nutrition nonprofit based in London, points out that BMI does not reflect the presence of abdominal fat that can hamper the body's organs. She says BMI does not distinguish between body fat and muscle mass. Muscle mass is built through exercise and is considered desirable by most people. But since muscle tissue is heavier than fat tissue, a person who has developed substantial musculature would have a higher BMI than a person who does not. Writes medical journalist Christian Nordqvist in the journal *Medical News Today*, "BMI will inevitably class muscly, athletic people as fatter than they really are."[8] BMI also does not account for bone mass—an important factor in determining the proper BMI for children because they are constantly growing and, therefore, their bone mass is constantly changing.

Furthermore, as children continue to weigh more as a group, future comparisons may lead to underreporting the obesity problem. Write Jacob C. Warren and K. Bryant Smalley,

> The troubling aspect of these definitions is that they're based on population norms, meaning that the more overweight a population is as a whole, the less children will

actually be classified as overweight or obese (since the definition is based on comparisons to others). This comparative nature of the definition of childhood obesity has disguised the gradual shift in children's weight leading us to the point we have reached today.[9]

Who Is Affected by Obesity?

According to the CDC, as of 2014, about 12 to 18 percent of American children and teens had BMIs high enough to be considered obese. Together, they represent 12.7 million young people grappling with excess weight. But the obesity epidemic seems to be hitting some segments of children and adolescents harder than others, CDC data suggest. For example, Hispanic teens and children have the highest rates of obesity of any ethnicity, nearly 22 percent. Almost as high are the rates for black teens and children, at nearly 20 percent. Young white people have average obesity rates of 14.7 percent, while the lowest obesity rate, 8.6 percent, is found among Asian American young people.

A person's chance of becoming obese rises as he or she grows older. That is because weight is often put on over time, and the older one gets the more freedom one has to eat meals away from home. Often that means choosing less nutritional options for meals, usually obtained through fast-food restaurants. According to the CDC, 8.9 percent of two- to five-year-olds were obese in 2014. Among their slightly older peers, those who are six to eleven, the rates had climbed to 17.5 percent, topping off at 20.5 percent for twelve- to nineteen-year-olds.

Obesity affects both boys and girls, but there are some indications suggesting that boys are more at risk than girls. A 2016 study published in the medical journal the *Lancet* analyzed BMI data from more than 130 million five- to nineteen-year-olds from around the world. Among its findings were that from 1975 to 2016, the number of obese girls rose from 5 million to 50 million.

Childhood Obesity Is Costly

There are plenty of good reasons why childhood obesity needs to be addressed. Seldom discussed, however, are the costs associated with the disease.

Researchers at Duke University in North Carolina calculated how much more it costs to raise an obese child than one of normal weight. The researchers concluded that an obese child racks up an additional $19,000 in health care expenses over his or her childhood years for such needs as increased doctor visits and medication required to treat various obesity-related illnesses. Using that figure, they were able to estimate that the total health care bill for all obese children who grow into adulthood in the United States is $14 billion, a sum borne by parents, health insurance companies, and the government. Adding to that but not calculated are costs shouldered by corporations whose obese employees may require more sick days or perform their jobs less well when they are feeling ill.

Duke University professor Eric Andrew Finkelstein, who led the study, says, "Reducing childhood obesity is a public health priority that has substantial health and economic benefits."

Quoted in Duke Global Health Institute, "Over a Lifetime, Childhood Obesity Costs $19,000 per Child," April 7, 2014. https://globalhealth.duke.edu.

During the same period, the number of obese boys jumped from 6 million to 74 million. The study did not address why there was a bigger increase in obesity among boys than girls. But what boys and girls have in common is that they all started out with baby fat.

Baby Fat

Baby fat is part of what makes babies cute. But baby fat has a purpose—it helps babies store energy. Chubby thighs, round tummies, and pudgy faces are all manifestations of baby fat. Baby fat can also confuse parents. Typical parents expect their babies to have some baby fat, and this expectation is generally not a problem. Yet it becomes an issue when parents look at their overweight or obese children and believe that what they are seeing is just a baby fat phase their child will outgrow. In truth, babies are supposed to start losing their baby fat when they become toddlers, about nine months after their births—a time when they become more active as they learn how to crawl and walk. Therefore, parents who see their young children maintaining extra weight as they grow into toddlers and beyond are wrong to assume it is simply harmless baby fat.

For example, researchers at Emory University in Atlanta, Georgia, examined data from a pool of more than seventy-seven hundred students who had their heights and weights recorded on seven occasions from their kindergarten years through the eighth grade. In 2014, when the researchers reported their study results,

Fat on a baby has a purpose: it helps the baby's body store energy. Once babies become more active—when they reach the stage of crawling and walking—they usually begin to lose baby fat.

they found that 13 percent of children in kindergarten were obese and 15 percent were overweight—a period in their lives more than four years after they were supposed to have lost their baby fat. The study also found that children who were overweight in kindergarten were four times as likely to be overweight in middle school. In fact, according to the study, 21 percent of the eighth-grade students were obese while 17 percent were overweight.

Says Edward Abramson, a clinical psychologist at California State University in Chico, California, "Kids go through growth spurts and develop at different rates so it's easy to assume that a 'chubby' child just has too much baby fat, and with time will just outgrow it and become a normal weight teen and adult. Unfortunately, this is the exception rather than the rule."[10]

> "It's easy to assume that a 'chubby' child just has too much baby fat, and with time will just outgrow it and become a normal weight teen and adult. Unfortunately, this is the exception rather than the rule."[10]
>
> —Edward Abramson, California State University psychologist

So parents of children as young as kindergarten age need to pay attention to how their children are doing with respect to weight gain.

A Disease That Progresses

As the Emory University study shows, if left unchecked, obesity can progress through childhood and beyond. William Dietz, a nutrition expert at the George Washington University in Washington, DC, asserts that "kids who already have obesity seem to be getting more severe."[11] In fact, Dietz says, at least 6 million teens and adolescents may already have the most severe form of obesity, which is known as morbid obesity. Morbid obesity is defined as having a BMI over forty.

Says Asheley Skinner, also a nutritionist at the George Washington University, "Kids with more severe forms of obesity are first developing obesity at younger ages and it gets worse and worse over time. We live in a world where kids aren't as active and it's easy for obesity to get continuously worse."[12]

Excess body fat can lead to severe health consequences, even for people not yet out of their teenage years. Among those consequences are heart disease, cancer, asthma, and joint problems. Also, in the most extreme form, people who are morbidly obese may have great difficulty moving around, may be bedbound, require breathing machines, and even need assistance with all facets of their daily lives—such as bathing and using the toilet.

Of course, not everyone who is obese has the medical problems typically associated with carrying too much weight. Also, certainly, there are people who have normal BMIs who suffer from various illnesses. This seeming contradiction has led some people to suggest that it is possible to be fat and healthy.

The "Fat and Healthy" Debate

There are people who are slim who nevertheless have high blood pressure, diabetes, or high cholesterol, for example. Science journalist Sara Chodosh contends that overweight and obese people are not necessarily unhealthy people. She says,

The "fat but fit" debate has been raging for years now, and it's certainly far from over. That being said, a lot of research is in—and so far it said that overweight people can absolutely be healthier than thin people who don't exercise. That's not to say that everyone with extra fat who works out is in better shape than every lazy person who never hits the gym. . . . There are [also] plenty of people who don't work out but who are nevertheless in perfect shape. Just like there are fat people who have excellent health markers and don't end up with heart problems.[13]

Robert Gilchick, chairman of the AMA Council on Science and Public Health, takes this even further. He is troubled by referring to

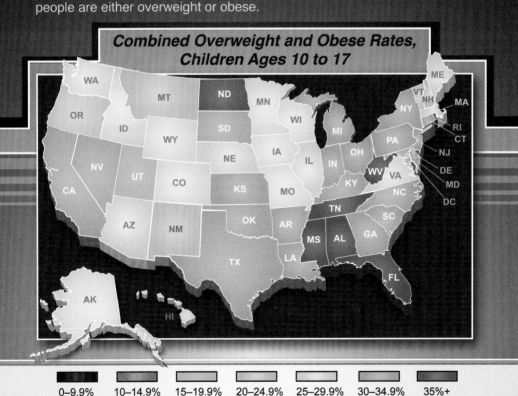

Overweight and Obese Young People, Ages 10–17

Statistics compiled from the National Survey of Children's Health in 2016 show the rates of overweight and obese young people in each state. The state with the least number of overweight or obese young people was Utah, with about 19 percent, while Tennessee had the highest rate, at nearly 38 percent. Overall, the survey found, about 31 percent of American young people are either overweight or obese.

Combined Overweight and Obese Rates, Children Ages 10 to 17

0–9.9%   10–14.9%   15–19.9%   20–24.9%   25–29.9%   30–34.9%   35%+

Source: Trust for America's Health and Robert Wood Johnson Foundation, "The State of Obesity: Better Policies for a Healthier America," September 2017. https://stateofobesity.org.

obesity as a disease. He says, "Why should one-third of Americans be diagnosed as having a disease if they aren't necessarily sick?"[14]

Perhaps researchers from Imperial College London and Cambridge University in Great Britain settled the debate with their 2017 study of more than a half-million Europeans. The study followed people from ten European countries for twelve years and concluded that people who are overweight or obese have nearly a 30 percent higher risk of developing heart disease than people who maintain healthy weights. This association was true even if the overweight people had normal blood pressure, blood sugar, and

Obesity: A Threat to National Security

As more and more young people in America grow into obese young adults, leaders of the country's armed forces worry that this disturbing trend might eventually affect the United States' ability to defend itself. Teens can enlist in the military at eighteen (or seventeen, if their parents give them permission), but according to the military, about 31 percent of young people who want to enlist are turned down because they weigh too much.

Carrying extra weight can make people less able to move quickly, carry heavy equipment, and walk for miles under tough conditions—all situations that can come up in combat. In addition, if a man or woman is wounded in battle, it would be more difficult to carry the wounded out of harm's way if he or she is obese.

Mark Hertling, a retired US Army general, believes the issue of teenage obesity must be addressed if the US military is expected to maintain an effective fighting force. He says, "Over the last decade, we have experienced increasing difficulty in recruiting soldiers due to the decline in the health of our nation's youth. Unless we see significant change in physical activity and nutrition in America our national security will be affected." Adds John Troxell, sergeant major of the US Army Command, "If I have to climb up to the top of a mountain in Nuristan, in Afghanistan, and if I have someone who is classified as clinically obese, they are potentially going to be a liability for me on that patrol."

Quoted in US Centers for Disease Control and Prevention, "Unfit to Serve: Obesity Is Impacting National Security." www.cdc.gov.

Quoted in Andrew Tilghman, "The U.S. Military Has a Huge Problem with Obesity and It's Only Getting Worse," *Military Times*, September 11, 2016. www.militarytimes.com.

cholesterol. Camille Lassale, who led the study, says, "Our findings challenge the concept of the 'healthy obese.' . . . Our findings show that if a patient is overweight or obese, all efforts should be made to help them get back to a healthy weight. Even if their blood pressure, blood sugar and cholesterol appear within the normal range, excess weight is still a risk factor."[15]

"Why should one-third of Americans be diagnosed as having a disease if they aren't necessarily sick?"[14]

—Robert Gilchick, chairman of the AMA Council on Science and Public Health

The same year that the European study was released also brought an important announcement from the US Preventive Services Task Force. Appointed by HHS, the task force called for all American children between six and eighteen to be screened for obesity. The task force is convinced that there is a benefit to identifying such children early on and helping their parents find the resources they need to begin dealing with the underlying issues that lead to unhealthy weight gain.

Attitudes about obesity have changed from the time when excess pounds used to indicate that the bearer was wealthy and influential. Today, overweight and obese individuals are uniformly advised to lose weight to avoid suffering adverse health consequences. Even children as young as kindergarten age are being screened because over time obesity tends to worsen and become more difficult to conquer.

Chapter 2

What Causes Obesity?

ood provides all living beings with the energy they need to grow and survive, but not all food is the same. That energy is measured in calories—units of heat produced when food is burned by the body as fuel. A slice of chocolate cake has a lot of calories—depending on the recipe, the amount of icing and, of course, the size of the slice—perhaps as many as 350 calories. On the other hand, a stalk of celery has about 6 calories. It means that somebody who eats a slice of chocolate cake for dessert has to be very active after the meal to burn all 350 calories from that piece of cake. Otherwise, the calories that are not burned will be stored in the body as fat. And if that person eats another piece of chocolate cake the next day, and does not find a way to burn all the calories from that slice, then the extra calories will again be turned into fat. And on and on it will go, perhaps eventually turning that chocolate cake lover into an obese person.

On the other hand, the person who consumed the stalk of celery for lunch would ordinarily have little trouble burning those calories. And if that person who eats the celery stalk for lunch is dieting and hoping to lose weight, that will probably happen.

That person's body will need energy and will turn to burning stored fat to meet the body's need.

Therefore, obesity often occurs when individuals consume more calories than they need to meet their energy needs. Today, more people are exceeding that number than in past decades. Says Sujit Sharma, a pediatric emergency room physician in Atlanta, Georgia, "On average, we consume more calories than we did just 30 years ago, without a corresponding biological need for more calories. Between 1971 and 1974, the average American adult consumed almost exactly 2,000 calories per day. Thirty years later, that number increased to more than 2,200 calories."[16] Certainly, an extra two hundred calories a day does not sound like that many more calories, but many people are consuming those extra calories 365 days a year, year after year, and not taking steps to burn those calories. In other words, they are not exercising enough.

> "On average, we consume more calories than we did just 30 years ago, without a corresponding biological need for more calories."[16]
>
> —Sujit Sharma, a pediatric emergency room physician in Atlanta, Georgia

Fast and Slow Metabolisms

But eating too many calories and not exercising enough to burn them before they turn into fat does not tell the whole story. There is also a biological element to how people burn calories that is unique to every person. Not all people burn calories at the same rate. How quickly and easily they burn calories depends a great deal on their metabolisms. The metabolism is the natural ability of a person's cells to absorb and burn calories. It is a trait ordinarily inherited from one's parents, meaning it is genetic in nature. In other words, some people are born with faster metabolisms, while some are born with slower metabolisms.

That is why some people seem to be natural athletes—athletic performance comes easy to them because they were born

Champion Olympic swimmer Michael Phelps competes in the 200-meter butterfly event. People who have fast metabolisms tend to excel at sports.

with fast metabolisms. They burn calories easily and, therefore, their bodies remain in top shape to compete in sports. Says science writer Richard Alleyne, "Super fit athletes burn more energy than couch potatoes even when they are resting. . . . Endurance-trained athletes have a higher resting muscle metabolism than their unfit counterparts, suggesting that they burn energy faster than sedentary people even without exercising."[17]

As for those born with slow metabolisms, they have inherited a trait that makes it more difficult for their cells to absorb and burn calories. That does not mean people with slow metabolisms cannot excel in sports—but they have to work harder to do it than people who were born with fast metabolisms.

Loss of Willpower

Slow metabolisms are only partially to blame for the obesity epidemic. It is a combination of many factors that lead people to gain weight. Scientists have pointed to such factors as parental influence, genetics, the rapid growth of the fast-food industry, increases in portion size, and the sedentary behavior of many people as reasons for the obesity epidemic. For example, it is no secret that many young people today spend an exorbitant amount of time staring at their smartphones or manipulating the controls on their video games. A generation ago, instead of playing on their Xboxes (which, after all, did not exist), young people may have been spending more of their free time after school at the neighborhood basketball court.

Another contributing factor is a lack of willpower—the ability to say no to an extra slice of chocolate cake for dessert. Irrespective of how much fat individuals may be carrying on their bodies, they all have one biological trait that has not changed over the course of human history, which is that bodies work the same way today as they have in the past. In other words, the human body burns fat the same way in the twenty-first century as it did in the tenth century. In today's world, human cells still absorb and burn calories the same way they did two thousand, ten thousand, or twenty thousand years ago.

What has changed, though, is how the brain reacts to food. Experts wonder whether people today simply have less willpower—that is, the self-discipline to limit their intake of crave-worthy foods that are high in calories and low in nutritional value. In fact, a 2014 study by the California Institute of Technology found that when faced with selecting two choices for a meal—a tasty dessert high in calories or a nutritional dish low in calories—people are 10 percent more likely to pick the tasty dessert. "Taste versus health . . . is a trade-off we are often faced with when deciding what to eat," says Peter A. Ubel, a behavioral scientist at Duke University in North Carolina. "Some foods are bad for our health but happen to taste quite good. All of us have limited willpower, and . . . those unhealthy foods become harder to resist."[18] Moreover, scientists have long established that young people's brains are not fully developed until they reach their twenties, meaning that as teenagers they often make rash decisions without thinking of the consequences. Certainly, one rash decision that can easily be made is the decision to have an extra slice of chocolate cake. If teenagers also lack willpower, then it is easy to see why they may be consuming too many calories and finding themselves on the road to obesity.

The Body Protects Itself

But people who manage to ramp up their willpower, hoping that will help them resist the chocolate cake, may find another formidable opponent blocking their desire to stay fit: the human body's protective mechanism that kicks in when it is hungry. Sandra Aamodt, a neuroscientist and nutritional expert, says the body possesses a sort of internal thermostat that kicks in when a person's weight goes above or below where it typically resides. In other words, the body has become used to the weight it usually carries and often causes a reaction when that weight suddenly fluctuates from the norm.

So when an obese person tries to lose weight by eating less, his or her body is likely to respond by slowing down the speed with which calories are burned. "That's probably just a biological response to repeated starvation,"[19] says Aamodt.

Joy Manning, former nutrition editor for the healthy-living journal *Prevention*, says, "If only you had more willpower, you would easily stick to your diet or exercise program, right? Nope. It turns out you need a lot more than willpower to do things like that. It's not just about self-control. In fact, willpower might be the most misunderstood of virtues."[20]

Parental Influence

Young people need more than just willpower to overcome their rash decisions to gorge on Doritos or their body's defensive mechanism that tells the body it is hungry and needs to eat. Parents

Do Teens Know What Makes Them Fat?

Many teens are aware of the issues that surround obesity, according to a 2013 poll sponsored by the National Basketball Association. Asked to explain why children become overweight, 54 percent of the twelve hundred girls and boys polled by the organization pointed to the lack of exercise and eating unhealthful foods. An equal number of respondents said that they worried about their weight, and 4 percent acknowledged being overweight.

Many of the young people who participated in the poll had already taken steps to control their weight. The most popular way they selected was to exercise more and choose healthier foods. Sixty-four percent of children and teens said they pursue more exercise and healthier eating habits. Another 17 percent had tried dieting, 14 percent made a point of eating fewer meals in restaurants, and 5 percent used medication.

The young poll participants also had a good grasp of resources they could turn to if they wanted to reduce their weight. The most popular way was to find a group that promotes physical fitness (27 percent), but other options named included watching healthful cooking demonstrations (16 percent), getting help from parents (15 percent), and making use of information available at school (8 percent).

play an important role in the futures of their sons and daughters—including futures that may be plagued by obesity.

Parents determine what foods children find available at home, how often they eat out, and where their food dollars are spent. The association between parents and weight gain in their children may even begin in the womb, as one 2016 study of forty-three hundred mothers and their seventy-eight hundred children suggested. The study sought to determine whether mothers who gained excessive weight during pregnancy had larger-than-average babies and whether those babies were more likely to become overweight children. Such an association was found and reported in the medical journal *Pediatric Obesity*: "The results of this study suggest that 'overnutrition' in pregnancy independently affects child body composition throughout child development."[21]

In other words, many women who eat too much during pregnancy are likely to pass on the extra fat to their babies. And, eventually, those babies might not be able to shed the fat as ordinary newborns eventually do. Instead, they carry the extra weight with them as they grow older. The study's authors suggest that discouraging pregnant women from gaining more weight than necessary to support the fetus might result in fewer overweight children.

As babies grow, they develop their own unique nutritional patterns. There is little doubt that family members who eat at home and cook their own meals instead of running out to nearby fast-food restaurants several times a week are less likely to be battling obesity.

In addition to laying down the ground rules on meals, parents also provide their offspring with their DNA, passing on genes that may be associated with fatness or thinness. Simply put, many young people inherit the physiology of their parents or other relatives. That could help explain why everybody in a household

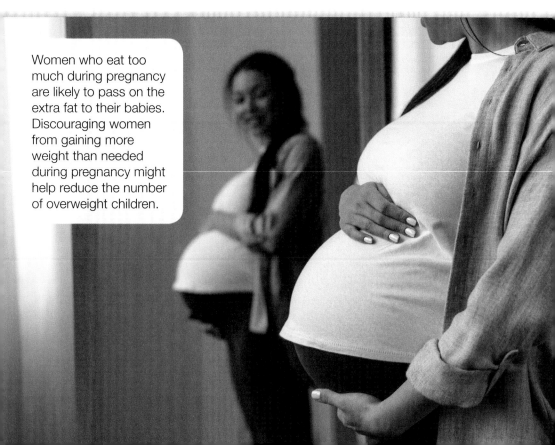

Women who eat too much during pregnancy are likely to pass on the extra fat to their babies. Discouraging women from gaining more weight than needed during pregnancy might help reduce the number of overweight children.

seems to be obese—or seems to be super athletes. But that is hardly the rule—the CDC estimates that only about 5 percent of cases of childhood obesity are caused by genetic factors.

Impact of Fast Food

Genetic factors may play a small role in determining who is obese, but anybody who has walked around the typical American neighborhood can find a much more obvious reason for the obesity epidemic: the abundance of fast-food restaurants available that serve low-cost meals. Experts agree such meals for the most part lack an emphasis on good nutrition.

Forty years ago, before the obesity epidemic began, fast-food restaurants were far less common than they are today. According to the market research website Statista.com, in 1970, Americans spent $6 billion on fast food. By 2020, Americans are expected to spend $223 billion.

Anyone who watches television could be tempted to go out—or ask their parents to take them out—to grab one of the offerings from McDonald's $1 menu or $3 Happy Meals with toys associated with upcoming kids' movies. They might also be tempted by Hardee's $4 meal that comes with a cheeseburger, fried chicken sandwich, fries, and a soft drink. The $4 meal seems like a great deal—all that food for little money—but it also has a high-calorie surprise. An adult who consumes all of the food in the Hardee's $4 meal will be consuming 1,420 calories—about two-thirds of a day's recommended intake.

Moreover, advertising for fast food invariably shows families having a good time as they eat. Says Sharma, "All of us, adults and children alike, are constantly bombarded with messages that consciously and unconsciously influence our decision-making. We think people in the ad seem happy, so why not follow suit?"[22]

Eric Schlosser, a journalist who has probed the fast-food industry, says companies like McDonald's have a tremendous influence on Americans' diet and culture. He contends that the company's corporate symbol, the golden arches, as well as the company mascot, the clown Ronald McDonald, have arguably become the most familiar symbols in American society. Schlosser adds,

> McDonald's spends more money on advertising and marketing than any other brand. As a result, it has replaced Coca-Cola as the world's most famous brand. McDonald's operates more playgrounds than any other private entity in the United States. It is one of the nation's largest distributors of toys. A survey of American school children found that 96 percent could identify Ronald McDonald. The only fictional character with a higher degree of recognition was Santa Claus.[23]

Healthier Happy Meals

It is easy to see why fast food is so desirable. Schlosser says the average preschooler sees three commercials touting the deliciousness of fast food each day while older siblings view as many as five fast-food commercials. Yet, clearly more than watching is taking place. According to a 2015 report from the US National Center for Health Statistics, more than 33 percent of American teens and children eat fast food on any given day. More telling, among those who eat fast food, some 12 percent are getting 40 percent of their calories from those meals.

In recent years the fast-food industry has taken some steps to add healthier alternatives to their menus. It is possible to order a salad at McDonald's or to have a Happy Meal that comes with an apple instead of cookies and nonfat milk instead of sugary

"A survey of American school children found that 96 percent could identify Ronald McDonald. The only fictional character with a higher degree of recognition was Santa Claus."[23]

—Journalist Eric Schlosser

People with Prader-Willi Syndrome Can't Stop Eating

Jacob Yashinsky, twenty-six, lives in Toronto, Canada, where he runs his own jewelry business. But because of a rare disease with which he was born, Yashinsky often finds himself thinking about food—even after he has just eaten. He has Prader-Willi syndrome, a disease afflicting about thirty thousand people worldwide. Its symptoms include the desire to constantly eat and the sense of never feeling full. Among patients, their slowed metabolism often leads to obesity. If they are not careful, Prader-Willi sufferers can actually eat themselves to death. Some people with Prader-Willi also have development delays that make them unable to live independently even when they reach Yashinsky's age. Fortunately, that is not the case for him, and he has even been able to lose nearly forty pounds by carefully watching what he eats.

Merlin G. Butler, a psychology professor at the University of Kansas, notes that "there is no cure right now. . . . The most effective treatment is keeping away from food sources, even if that means padlocking refrigerators and pantries. They have to be watched closely."

Yashinsky describes what it feels like to have Prader-Willi. He says, "I feel like if I don't eat, I'm going to starve, even though I eat pretty frequently every day. It's very difficult. It's not psychological hunger, it's physical hunger."

Quoted in Nick Rose, "A Rare Eating Disorder Causes Binge Eating and Food Theft," Munchies, November 27, 2015. https://munchies.vice.com.

soda. But as well-intentioned as those efforts may be, those offerings are most likely not among the more popular choices people make. Admitting as much is Andrew Puzder, former chief executive officer (CEO) of the company that owns Hardee's and Carl's Jr. "We have wonderful, healthy foods if people want to buy them," Puzder says. "But they don't sell particularly well."[24]

Sugary Beverages

Invariably, a fast-food meal is accompanied with a soda—a beverage high in sugar and, therefore, high in calories. In fact, the typical twenty-ounce cup of soda contains 240 calories. But sodas are not the only beverages cited as culprits in the obesity epidemic. Many juices, energy drinks, sports drinks, and sweetened ice teas also have high sugar contents and have been singled out for their roles in contributing to obesity. Certainly, many of these beverages are consumed at fast-food restaurants where they represent significant profits for the restaurant chains. This may explain why McDonald's sells more Coca-Cola than any other business in the world, according to Schlosser.

Just as with fast food, the beverage industry spends considerable money advertising its products to children and adults. According to a 2014 fact sheet on sugared beverages marketed to youths, compiled by the Rudd Center for Food Policy and Obesity, in 2010 teenagers were exposed to more than four hundred ads for sodas and energy drinks that year—that is more than one every day. The center also found that the typical teenager absorbs 226 calories a day from sugary beverages, which are more calories than they absorb from a typical portion of pizza.

Experts say that sugary beverages have a sneaky effect on people's diets. Since they taste good and are not particularly filling, it is easy for people to consume more calories than they realize. Meanwhile, those who drink one or two cans of soda daily increase their risk of developing diabetes by more than 26 percent, according to a 2012 fact sheet put out by the Harvard University School of Public Health.

Multiple studies that have linked obesity with the consumption of sugary drinks include one study that examined the effect of drinking such beverages on the weight of eleven-year-old children in Massachusetts. The 2001 study found that for each additional twelve-ounce soda consumed by a child each day, the odds of becoming obese increased by 60 percent during the nineteen months the children were followed.

Experts blame the obesity epidemic on a variety of factors, including the abundance of fast-food restaurants. Prominent advertising, toy promotions, low prices, and convenience contribute to the popularity of fast-food restaurants.

Lack of Exercise

Sugary drinks and fast food high in calories may contribute to obesity, but research has shown that while people are consuming more and more fattening foods and beverages, they are also spending less time in activities that would help burn those calories before they turn into fat. Inactivity causes bodies to expend less energy and store more fat. For example, spending a lot of time watching TV, which may also include snacking, contributes to weight gain.

In 2015 the American Academy of Pediatrics, a professional association for physicians who specialize in the health of children, recommended that children and teens spend less than two hours a day in front of the television and other devices with screens; more than that is likely to contribute to excess weight gain and obesity. Young people should also pay attention to how much time they spend being active each day, setting a goal of at least one hour a day, which is the recommendation of the World Health Organization (WHO). One WHO study, released in 2017, tracked activity levels for nearly thirteen thousand individuals ages six to eighty-four. The study revealed the shocking findings that nineteen-year-olds are no more active than sixty-year-olds. "It was definitely a big surprise,"[25] says Vadim Zipunnikov, a biostatistician at Johns Hopkins University in Baltimore, Maryland, and leader of the study. Among the study's other findings were that few children and teens were getting the recommended one hour of moderate to vigorous daily exercise recommended by WHO. Twenty-five percent of boys between ages six and eleven and 50 percent of girls that age were not active for an hour. As for teens, half the boys and 75 percent of teen girls also failed to reach one hour of recommended exercise each day.

Clearly, eating too much, exercising too little, and consuming sugary beverages and fast food high in calories have all contributed to the obesity epidemic. And while experts may disagree on which factors are mostly responsible for making people obese, there is no question that those who weigh too much for their own good are probably guilty of engaging in most if not all of the causes of obesity.

Chapter 3

What Is It Like to Live with Obesity?

When Chris McGann was fifteen, he watched his friends load up on pizza and desserts in their middle school cafeteria. McGann, who struggled with his weight, knew that he should not eat what they were eating. It did not seem fair that his body did not behave as theirs did. He says, "My friends eat the pizza and the Little Debbie cakes and they're all as thin as rails. It's really hard to walk by that stuff because it looks so good. I just think I want to be healthy, I want to lose weight and I know if I eat those things it's not going to happen."[26]

McGann and others coping with obesity know they are different. Their schoolmates and other people may not let them forget it. As a result, childhood obesity often brings with it a host of social and mental health problems, including bullying, fat shaming, self-esteem issues, depression, anxiety, and poor school performance. In addition to the psychological and mental effects, physical ills can make daily life dangerous for those children and teens living with obesity.

Bullying and Fat Shaming

Young people develop self-esteem through interactions with their parents. But as teens, their views of themselves are more likely to reflect how their friends and peers see them. Obese teens, however, are more likely to have problems forming friendships than slimmer teens. This reality was reflected in a 2013 poll of 1,168 teens and children conducted on behalf of NBA/WNBA FIT, a health and wellness program sponsored by the National Basketball Association and Women's National Basketball Association. In that poll some 60 percent of the boys and girls surveyed thought that overweight children had a tougher time making friends than slender young people.

Research from Duke University shows that young people begin showing unconscious prejudice toward overweight people by the time they reach the age of nine. In their 2017 study, 114 children between the ages of nine and eleven were asked to view photographs of other children—some overweight and some not—doing everyday activities. Mixed in with the photos were other images considered neutral. The study participants were asked to rate these neutral images as either "good" or "bad." Researchers found that the children were more likely to rate the neutral images as bad if they were preceded by photographs of overweight students.

A 2011 study that appeared in the *Journal of School Health* found that 85 percent of teens had witnessed overweight classmates being teased in gym class—sometimes by their gym teachers. (In the same study a majority of students also said they had witnessed other overweight students being ignored, teased, and made the subjects of nasty rumors.) Moreover, in a 2013 study reported in the medical journal *Pediatrics*, 350 overweight teens were asked which groups of people teased or bullied them. Forty-two percent of the overweight teens said gym teachers and coaches had exhibited such behavior toward them. Meanwhile, 37 percent of the overweight kids said their own parents bullied them, under the assumption that their comments would motivate their children to lose weight.

Kim Kachmann-Geltz of Hilton Head, South Carolina, grew up with a father who often insulted her at the family dinner table. As a neurosurgeon, he was an educated man and his daughter looked up to him. Even so, Kachmann-Geltz's father would tell her that if she ate dessert, no man would ever want to marry her. She never forgot his hurtful comments. "My father's rants still must be stirring deep within my subconscious. Cognitively, I know the things he said weren't right or good. But somehow the truth still hasn't sunk in 100 percent,"[27] she says.

Sometimes a sibling does the fat shaming. "I guess it started when I was around four or five years old. I don't know," one obese teen writes on a social media network. "I just know that my older sister had been calling me names and ridiculing me from some point in my childhood until I turned about twelve years old. So naturally, I am used to being called fat and having people talk about me behind my back for a while now. . . . The point is, I'm fat, I'm fifteen and I hate it."[28]

Obese young people tend to have low self-esteem, depression, anxiety, and poor grades in school. Some are subjected to bullying and have trouble forming friendships.

Obesity and Mental Health

Constantly being called fat by friends, teachers, parents, and siblings has an effect on young people, often leading them to regard themselves with low self-esteem. A thirteen-year-old girl tells the *Guardian*, a British newspaper,

> I'm overweight for my age. . . . It's consumed my life. I can't go shopping with my friends in town because I can't let them know my clothing size. If I sit down I'm always conscious that I look fat. If I take off my coat I feel people judging my waist. I dread it when my mother buys me clothes and I have to fake a smile to not upset her, all the while knowing the clothes will be bigger than hers. It takes up everything: my whole life revolves around how I look to other people.[29]

Moreover, constantly being bullied or fat-shamed can lead to mental illness in children and teens. Obesity is believed to be a leading cause of anxiety and depression. (Anxiety is defined as constant nervousness or feelings of unease; depression is a prolonged feeling of sadness, lack of energy, and desire to remain secluded from others.) Depression and anxiety are often caused by low self-esteem. And since children and teens who feel shame about their bodies are likely to have low self-esteem, they are candidates for anxiety and depression. "Many teens have trouble separating how they feel about their bodies with how they feel about themselves as people," says Falls Church, Virginia, pediatrician Nicolas Stettler. "Those who don't like their bodies, for whatever reasons, often have trouble liking themselves."[30]

One twenty-four-year-old woman, obese since childhood, wrote about her depression on a website maintained by Recovery.org, an organization that assists people in finding help for mental illness and substance abuse:

> I'm morbidly obese. I weigh 260 pounds (118 kg). I have no job and go to school two days a week. I'm an avid proponent of escapism. I'm into watching movies and TV shows.

I am obsessed with reading romantic fiction because I know no man will love me. . . . I am the oldest child in my family. I am 24 and I am a disappointment to parents. . . . I'm terrified of going to social functions and have no ambition. I don't want people to see how fat I am. I don't want them to judge me on the fact that I go to a lower class college. I have no self-esteem. . . . I am very self-conscious. I can't tell anyone in person what my problems are as I fear judgment. I know for a fact that it's easy to figure out what I need to do. I need to wake up and experience life. I need to stop eating and exercise more. It's not rocket science. I need to apply myself in school and get a job. Despite knowing it all, I don't do anything about it.[31]

Hypertension

Obesity not only can lead to mental illnesses such as anxiety disorder and depression, but people who are obese are also likely to develop a raft of physical ills. Among them are high blood pressure, also known as hypertension, as well as type 2 diabetes, fatty liver disease, and sleep apnea.

Hypertension can lead to fatal consequences, such as heart attack and stroke. It is a common condition among obese people. Obese people often have higher levels of sodium in their blood, and they also retain more water in their bodies than slimmer individuals. The higher levels of water and sodium in the blood help drive blood pressure higher. Moreover, since obese people are large, their hearts need to work harder to pump the blood to their organs—this condition also leads to high blood pressure. And the arteries in the bodies of obese people frequently harden, making it harder for the heart to push the blood through the arteries, contributing to hypertension as well.

Anybody who has had a physical examination has undoubtedly had their blood pressure checked—it is a routine test, telling doctors a lot about a patient's health. Blood pressure is measured

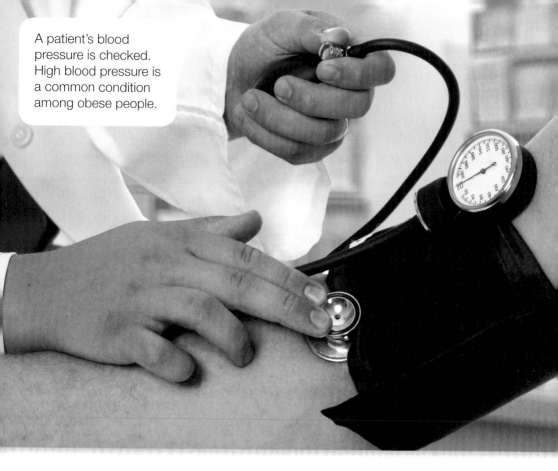

A patient's blood pressure is checked. High blood pressure is a common condition among obese people.

by a gauge that is attached to the arm by an inflatable cuff. The cuff reads the pressure and records it in the gauge, which contain a glass tube of mercury. The higher the blood pressure, the higher the mercury rises in the gauge.

Results are given in two numbers: systolic blood pressure and diastolic blood pressure. Systolic blood pressure measures how much pressure the blood exerts against the walls of the arteries when the heart is beating. Diastolic blood pressure measures how much pressure the blood exerts against artery walls between beats—in other words, when the heart is at rest. Physicians regard a normal blood pressure reading as "120 over 80," meaning the systolic blood pressure was recorded in the gauge at 120 millimeters of mercury, and the diastolic blood pressure was gauged at 80 millimeters of mercury.

The more pressure arteries are exposed to, the more likely those arteries are to become weak or damaged. Weakened arteries can lead to heart attacks and strokes as well as amputations, blindness, and other serious medical conditions.

Although physicians do not get concerned if the systolic and diastolic readings are a few points above average, obese people typically record blood pressure readings well above average numbers. (According to the CDC, high blood pressure starts at readings of 140 over 90.) That was the case with Cheyenne Cameron, sixteen, of Damon, Texas. Even before her blood pressure test, she knew she had a medical problem and needed to see a doctor. She recalls, "I felt like a car was sitting on my chest. Like a heavy chest pressure, and I was lightheaded. I felt horrible. I was helpless."[32] When Cameron's doctor took her blood pressure, she recorded very high numbers and was diagnosed with hypertension.

In fact, Cameron is among the 3.5 percent of young people in America diagnosed with hypertension—a problem that for many years was believed to only afflict adults. Before she knew what her problem was, Cameron frequently felt ill—so ill that she could not attend her freshman year of high school. At the time she weighed 220 pounds (99.8 kg) and was, therefore, obese. Cameron was able to lower her blood pressure by losing weight. She stopped eating fried foods and other foods with high calorie counts and managed to drop 60 pounds (27 kg). Eventually, her blood pressure dropped. She felt better and was able to return to school.

> "I felt like a car was sitting on my chest. Like a heavy chest pressure, and I was lightheaded. I felt horrible. I was helpless."[32]
>
> —Cheyenne Cameron, a sixteen-year-old hypertension patient

Type 2 Diabetes

In addition to hypertension, another ailment that is afflicting more and more young people is type 2 diabetes, which used to be referred to as adult-onset diabetes. But now, many youths are known to be developing the disease—and obesity is regarded as a primary cause. Type 2 diabetes occurs in young people when their bodies can no longer effectively process sugar in their blood. Their body's supply of insulin—the hormone responsible for breaking down sugar into energy their body can use—stops doing its job. As a result, excess sugar courses through the bloodstream where over time it can damage the heart, kidneys, eyes, and nerves. The longer a person has untreated type 2 diabetes, the more damage it is likely to do.

"This is not something we talked about 20 years ago and it is heartbreaking to think that now in this country there are about 20,000 children—children—who have Type 2 diabetes," says Tara Narula, professor of cardiovascular medicine at Hofstra University in Hempstead, New York. She adds, "We see the complications not when kids are 50 or 60—we're seeing this as early as five or 10 years down the road, when kids are now in the prime of their lives. They're starting jobs, they're in college, they're having families—and what's happening to them? They're developing end-stage [kidney] disease . . . heart attack and stroke."[33]

> "This is not something we talked about 20 years ago and it is heartbreaking to think that now in this country there are about 20,000 children—children—who have Type 2 diabetes."[33]
>
> —Tara Narula, professor of cardiovascular medicine at Hofstra University

Young people diagnosed with type 2 diabetes may need to take medication to regulate their blood sugar levels and change the way they eat to avoid spiking their blood sugar levels before and after meals. They may also need to engage in exercise, which improves the body's insulin sensitivity and makes it more effective at processing blood sugar. Additionally, they may need to monitor their blood sugar levels by pricking their finger to draw a speck of blood that can be analyzed by a meter, or have frequent blood tests ordered by their physicians. However, losing weight may be all that is needed to reverse the disease in young people.

Choosing to Be Called Fat

Many obese people have been hearing others refer to them as "fat" for virtually their entire lives. To be sure, it is used in a hurtful way. Now, however, some obese people believe they should embrace the word to make it less harmful.

Alysse Dalessandro, who designs clothing for larger women, is an activist who wishes overweight bodies were appreciated just as any other body type would be. "When I say that my body is fat, I am removing the power that it's held over me in the past as an insult," Dalessandro says. "It's literally just a description of the size of my body—'fat' doesn't mean ugly; 'fat' doesn't mean worthless. When we take back the word and say, 'Yeah, I'm fat and that's OK,' we're kind of taking that power away from it."

Cat Polivoda agrees. Polivoda is the cofounder of an organization that helps people accept their bodies called Body Brave, and often refers to herself as fat. She says,

> There is an element of reclaiming the word that I love. . . . I am comfortable with using the word. For instance, when people insist that I am "not fat" but I am, instead, "beautiful," I can remind them that I am both "fat and beautiful." Of course, "fat" is a very loaded term, and everyone gets to decide what words they want to use to describe themselves or with which to identify.

Quoted in Caroline Thompson, "Fat-Positive Activists Explain What It's Really Like to Be Fat," Vice.com, May 4, 2017. www.vice.com.

Heart Disease

Type 2 diabetes can have significant consequences, but of all diseases that can potentially take people's lives, heart disease is the number one killer. According to the CDC, about six hundred thousand Americans die from heart disease each year. It is a disease that usually progresses slowly over time, leading to heart failure caused by the gradual buildup of plaque. A sticky substance, plaque builds up on the walls of the arteries, narrowing them so that less blood can pass through them. Therefore, the heart has to work harder to supply blood to vital organs. Fat in the blood is

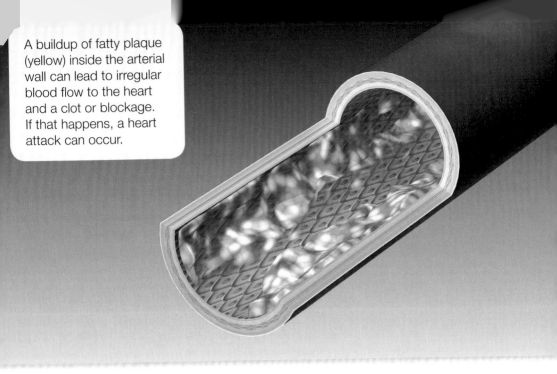

A buildup of fatty plaque (yellow) inside the arterial wall can lead to irregular blood flow to the heart and a clot or blockage. If that happens, a heart attack can occur.

one of the building blocks of plaque. Thanks to the obesity epidemic, physicians are starting to see younger patients with heart disease caused by plaque buildup in their arteries.

"Plaque buildup really starts from the time you are born, it's how fast it progresses that determines whether you're going to have heart disease or not," says Michael Langiulli, a cardiologist in Shreveport, Louisiana.

I can say that in the last 5 to 10 years, I've seen my share of 30-year-olds who come in with heart attacks, who come in with . . . weak hearts, and that has to do mostly with their habits. Most of the people I see in their 30s and early 40s who have heart problems usually have been smoking since they were teenagers. They don't exercise. They eat a non-healthy diet.[34]

Fatty Liver Disease

The heart is not the only organ that can be affected by obesity. An overabundance of fat can also wreak havoc with the liver—an organ whose functions include converting fat into energy. But obesity often overwhelms the liver with fat, swelling the organ beyond its normal size. In many cases, the condition causes intense pain. "It's like you're being stabbed in your stomach with a knife,"[35] says

Gavin Owenby of Hiawassee, Georgia. He was diagnosed with fatty liver disease when he was thirteen.

To shrink his liver back down to normal size, Owenby was advised to lose weight. In some cases, though, the liver is permanently damaged and the only recourse is a liver transplant. That's what Julio needed. The teen from west Texas had been diagnosed with fatty liver disease; his liver's function was so compromised that it could not do its job.

At the time Julio was diagnosed with fatty liver disease he was morbidly obese, weighing some 400 pounds (181 kg). His daily habits included drinking a half-gallon (1.9 liters) of soda.

Poor School Performance

It may seem surprising, but being obese appears to have an effect on students' grades—particularly on the math scores earned by girls. At least that was the conclusion of a 2012 study that examined the academic records of nearly sixty-three hundred children from kindergarten through fifth grade.

In the study, reported in the journal *Child Development*, children who were obese in kindergarten were more likely to have lower math scores than their peers from first grade on. Becky Hashim, a psychologist at Children's Hospital at Montefiore in New York City, suggests obese children may have poorer social skills because of their obesity. She says, "Feelings of sadness or loneliness or anxiety in and of themselves may get in the way of school performance. It may be more difficult to pay attention. These kids may be less likely to ask a question [in class]."

Quoted in Amanda Gardner, "Does Obesity Affect School Performance?," CNN, June 14, 2012. www.cnn.com.

Julio received a new liver. His doctors warned him not to go back to his old habits of overeating, but Julio could not help himself. Following the transplant, doctors started seeing signs that his new liver was developing fatty liver disease.

Robert H. Lustig, professor of pediatrics at the University of California, San Francisco, says most people who are diagnosed with fatty liver disease do recover, usually by changing their eating habits. However, he says, as many as 25 percent of fatty liver disease patients will either need a liver transplant or succumb to the disease. "When you do the math, that's one million Americans dying from a nutritional disease," he says. "Considering that this disease is completely preventable, this is a travesty."[36]

Obese young people often find themselves afflicted with a poor quality of life. They may face physical ills, including hypertension, liver disease, and type 2 diabetes. In addition to the physical ills, they may often face psychological damage stemming from taunts and bullying, fat shaming, self-loathing, and hurtful comments from people they should be able to depend on—parents, teachers, and siblings—who may be misguided about the best ways to help them lose weight.

Chapter 4

Can Obesity Be Treated?

When he was a sophomore at a Denver, Colorado, high school, Alan Gamez took a course that changed his life. It was not chemistry or calculus. It was an exercise, health, and wellness class that taught the then 270 pound (122 kg) teen the basics of nutrition and exercise. Today Gamez credits the class with the incentive and information he needed to remake his life and his body.

Before he had this knowledge, Gamez was comfortable eating eight meals a day, mostly filled with comfort foods his mother made for him. He had few friends, hated to look in the mirror, and refused to try out for the baseball team even though he loved the sport. By the time he reached his junior year, Gamez was consuming smaller amounts of food, eating more healthful meals, and exercising. He shed 100 pounds (45 kg), attracted a girlfriend, and earned an award for coping with adversity. He also made the baseball team. "My confidence went up drastically,"[37] he says.

Gamez's case illustrates how childhood obesity can be treated with weight-loss programs that include lifestyle changes and also that family support is crucial in making such changes. In helping to guide Gamez into a new lifestyle, his parents participated in the program by changing their own eating habits as well as the type of foods the family consumed.

Doctors Need to Do More

While Gamez benefited from a class at school, most obese young people are typically referred to weight-loss programs by family physicians. Many of these programs are affiliated with their local medical centers, meaning physicians are often familiar with the plans they offer.

> "Overall, despite the recognition of obesity as a chronic disease, we doctors still don't treat it this way in the clinical setting."[38]
>
> —Penn State associate professor of medicine Jennifer Kraschnewski

Too often, however, physicians do not make such referrals for a number of reasons. Among them are their reluctance to engage patients on the topic of their weight and the increasingly large numbers of their patients who are overweight or obese. For instance, it has been estimated that the average primary care physician counts about fifty obese individuals under his or her care. Furthermore, they may feel that success will elude their patients, anyway. Says Jennifer Kraschnewski, associate professor of medicine at Penn State,

Overall, despite the recognition of obesity as a chronic disease, we doctors still don't treat it this way in the clinical setting. If we do help patients with weight loss efforts, we then stand back and watch as they regain weight, and then try to re-engage them in additional weight loss efforts. Of patients who lose even 5 percent of their weight, our work has shown that 2 in 3 will regain weight within one year. It's important for us as [physicians] to start thinking about better approaches. We wouldn't treat someone's high blood pressure with a medication for only a year and then scratch our heads as to why their blood pressure is high again two years later.[38]

There are a few more obstacles to being enrolled in a weight-loss program: affordability and availability of services. Only about 60 percent of children's hospitals have programs that have all the elements needed to be effective, according to Harvard Medical School researchers.

Families Participate Together

One teenager whose doctor did refer her to a weight-loss program is Molly, whose family participated in a special program provided by Children's Hospital Colorado in Aurora. As part of the hospital's Shape Down program, Molly and her family were given instructions on how to remake their eating habits—specific guidelines were given on portion sizing, selecting vegetables for mealtime, and bumping up their daily exercise. With the guidance she received, Molly was able to shed the extra pounds she

A North Carolina teenager works out with her grandfather in a program that focuses on nutrition, exercise, and behavior as a means to improving health. Kids who have supportive families are more likely to overcome obesity.

"It's helpful to go slow. It's about simple goals. You don't have to get to a perfect weight in order to have the health benefits."[39]

—Stephen Daniels, chief pediatrician at Children's Hospital Colorado

carried that had led to her being bullied when she was younger.

Stephen Daniels, chief pediatrician at Children's Hospital Colorado, is extremely careful about how he addresses obesity with his clients. For example, *diet* and *weight loss* are words he avoids using. Instead, he says, "You have to understand what kinds of behaviors are leading to the problem and changes to take. It's helpful to go slow. It's about simple goals. You don't have to get to a perfect weight in order to have the health benefits."[39]

According to the Preventive Task Force of the US Department of Health and Human Services, the most effective programs are those in which children between the ages of eight and sixteen, and their families, receive a minimum of twenty-six hours of attention over a period of at least six months or for as long as a year. (The task force noted that, optimally, patients and their families should receive fifty-two hours of attention.) During that time, they are counseled by a team made up of physicians, nutritionists, social workers, and physical activity specialists.

"I approach the issue by focusing on a child's health rather than weight. The focus should be on lifestyle habits and making changes as a family to help support the child."[40]

—Rachel DeHaven, physical activity specialist at Children's Hospital of Philadelphia

Says Rachel DeHaven, a physical activity specialist at Children's Hospital of Philadelphia who works with obese young people and their families, "In my work, I approach the issue by focusing on a child's health rather than weight. The focus should be on lifestyle habits and making changes as a family to help support the child."[40]

Weight-Loss Drugs

Although programs like those conducted at Children's Hospital Colorado help young people shed weight, there is always a possibility that once they leave the programs they will regain the weight they have lost. In many cases it may be necessary for those patients to use weight-loss drugs.

While adults are often routinely prescribed medication to help them lose weight, there are far fewer drug options for young people—and none at all for patients under the age of twelve. For patients over the age of twelve who have not yet reached the age of eighteen, a single drug has been approved for them: orlistat. The drug belongs to a group of medications known as lipase inhibitors. (Lipase is a chemical produced in the pancreas that helps the body digest fats.) By taking the drug, a patient's body will absorb less fat from foods consumed—which optimally would help the individual lose weight. However, there is a downside to the drug: It also restricts the body's ability to absorb the vitamins found in food. That is why the drug is not prescribed for children whose bodies are still developing. Moreover, there can be unpleasant side effects such as stomachaches, increased heart rates, and high blood pressure. Adolescents who take the drug are encouraged to make modifications to their lifestyles as well—such as doing more exercise—and not just to rely on the drug itself to lose weight.

The drug has been found to have just a modest impact on obesity; according to the Preventive Task Force, orlistat can help teens lose perhaps just five or seven pounds. Medication is, therefore, neither a quick nor permanent treatment for childhood obesity because unless young people change their lifestyles, they are likely to gain the weight back after they stop taking the drug.

Weight-Loss Surgery

While drugs may provide just temporary and modest relief from obesity, surgery is likely to provide much more dramatic and long-lasting—if not permanent—relief. Surgery to treat obesity is known as bariatric surgery. (The term stems from the Greek word *baros*, which means weight.) Bariatric surgery is usually reserved for individuals who have tried to lose weight on their own multiple times with little success. As many as two thousand bariatric surgeries are performed on American teenagers each year.

The two most common forms of weight-loss surgery are gastric bypass and gastric sleeve, also called a sleeve gastrectomy. Both of these procedures greatly restrict how much food a person can eat. Gastric bypass accomplishes that goal by creating a pouch that will do the job the patient's stomach used to do. The "old" stomach remains in place but is bypassed by the reconfigured digestive system. With a gastric sleeve, the patient still uses his or her stomach, but surgeons remove much of the organ, surgically taking out more than 60 percent. Therefore, the size of the patient's stomach is reduced greatly, meaning it will take less food to provide the patient with a feeling of fullness.

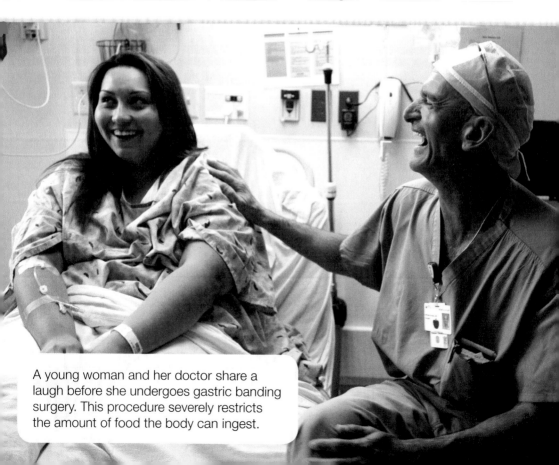

A young woman and her doctor share a laugh before she undergoes gastric banding surgery. This procedure severely restricts the amount of food the body can ingest.

Gastric bypass and gastric sleeve surgeries accounted for more than three-quarters of all bariatric surgeries from 2011 to 2015, according to the American Society for Metabolic and Bariatric Surgery, the professional association of physicians who perform the procedures. A less popular form of surgery is known as gastric banding surgery. In that procedure, a silicon ring—or band—is placed around the stomach, severely restricting how much food can be ingested. With the band in place, a patient can only eat about two tablespoons' worth of food at a time, whereas an unrestricted stomach can hold the equivalent of about sixty-four tablespoons. Moreover, patients with surgically implanted gastric bands need a lot of follow-up care: the bands may have to be adjusted as the patient's weight changes.

High Rates of Success

The surgery itself is only part of what is involved in living with a smaller, possibly redirected stomach. Medical practices that perform the surgery require potential participants to undergo a multistep and time-consuming process that can take between eight and fourteen months. For instance, the Adolescent Bariatric Program at Children's Hospital of Philadelphia is structured so that teens meet with nurse practitioners, dietitians, physical activity specialists, and social workers—in addition to their surgeons.

The team members must agree that surgery is the proper course for each individual and then prepare their patients for what life will be like postsurgery when continuing to eat as they had before would make them ill. In addition, in order to be considered for the program, patients must be between the ages of sixteen and twenty-one, have a BMI of more than fifty (or forty with high blood pressure, diabetes, sleep apnea, or fatty liver disease), be finished growing, and have a history of little progress in past supervised weight-loss programs.

Clearly, bariatric surgery takes a serious commitment to achieving weight loss by the patient—but there is no question that such surgeries have high rates of success. In 2016 the *New England Journal of Medicine* reported the results of a three-year study of 242 teenagers who had had bariatric surgery. Three years after their gastric bypass surgeries, the young patients had lost an average of 27 percent of their body weight. Teens who underwent sleeve gastrectomies lost 26 percent of their body weight. Perhaps more encouraging were the high rates of remission or even disappearance of weight-related problems. Many teens with diabetes, prediabetic conditions, and high blood pressure no longer had those issues.

Experts point out, however, that bariatric surgery is still a relatively new concept—the first gastric bypass was performed in 1994—and that more research is needed on the long-term effects of weight-loss surgery on young people. "The lingering question, however, is about the long-term consequences of such major surgery when performed on children and adolescents," write Jacob C. Warren and K. Bryant Smalley. "We simply don't know what they are yet, but that isn't preventing widespread increase in the surgeries."[41] Warren and Smalley are not fans of bariatric surgery because it involves using a medical procedure as a remedy for behavioral issues. They write, "Without corresponding intensive behavior change, weight losses will not be maintained, only increasing frustration."[42]

> "I was gaining 40 pounds a year. They told me unless something drastic happened, I would not see my 18th birthday."[43]
>
> —Sleeve gastrectomy patient Maria Caprigno

Nevertheless, Maria Caprigno is glad she had her sleeve gastrectomy. At the time she was fourteen and weighed 443 pounds (201 kg). Four years later, she had lost more than 130 pounds (59 kg). Still, having the surgery was a difficult decision for her and her family even though doctors warned them that Caprigno was on a dangerous path. "I was gaining 40 pounds a year. They told me unless something drastic happened, I would not see my 18th birthday."[43]

Before Caprigno's mother would let her have the surgery, she had the procedure herself to not only know what she was getting

World's Youngest Bariatric Surgery Patient

In 2013 history was made when the case of the youngest patient in the world to receive bariatric surgery became public. The child lived in Saudi Arabia and was just two years old.

Even at such a young age, the boy—whose name was not revealed—had already developed health problems due to obesity. He would stop breathing while asleep, and his legs were already turning inward, making him bowlegged. He weighed nearly 73 pounds (33 kg)—as much as a twelve-year-old.

At the time that the boy had more than 60 percent of his stomach surgically removed, he had already been under the care of an obesity clinic where two separate attempts to get him to lose weight failed. For example, when he weighed 47 pounds (21 kg), he was placed on a special diet. Instead of losing weight, he gained 17 pounds (8 kg).

After the boy had a sleeve gastrectomy, he instantly lost 20 pounds (9 kg). But because of his age and the substantial growth time ahead of him, physicians are concerned about what effect the surgery would have on his life. Australian diabetes specialist Paul Zimmet worries that a dangerous precedent may have been set. "It's going into unknown territory," he says. "We have no idea what effect this may have on the child's growth and unless he has proper follow up he may suffer vitamin deficiencies."

Quoted in Andy Berry, "Morbidly Obese BMI: Two-Year-Old Obese Boy in Saudi Arabia Becomes Youngest Person to Have Bariatric Surgery," *International Business Times*, September 19, 2013. www.ibtimes.com

her daughter into but to deal with her own obesity problem. "She told me she wasn't putting me under a knife that she hadn't been under herself," Caprigno recalls. "And I can't even imagine how difficult that decision was for her to allow me to do this."[44]

The Role Parents Play

Not every teenager or child who is obese has parents like Caprigno's, who are willing to help and who are knowledgeable about the best way to do so. In fact, well-meaning parents who are uninformed can actually make treatment of obesity harder than it already is.

Parents do their children a disservice when they constantly talk about their children's weight. Putting the focus on health rather than weight is smarter, with parents who are thoughtful about the entire family's habits having the edge over parents who focus only on the overweight child's food intake and exercise habits.

Parents should also make certain that their offspring have a sense of what is good about them—the things they do well and personality traits that make them special—instead of fixating on their body build. Finally, they need to pay attention to the attitudes they convey when they make negative comments about their own bodies and those of others. For example, when children are nearby, parents should not say a particular dress or pair of pants makes them feel fat or comment that a friend is looking poorly because she gained ten pounds.

Dianne Neumark-Sztainer, a weight researcher and professor at the University of Minnesota in Minneapolis, offers this advice to parents: "While getting dressed to go out, avoid making negative

Parents play a critical role in reducing childhood obesity. They need to intervene early, encouraging healthful eating before obesity occurs and helping their children develop new habits if and when obesity seems likely.

Teens with Eating Disorders May Fear Being Overweight

Teens are known for being hard on themselves when they have trouble fitting in. Some young men and women zero in on their weight to the point of obsession, developing the eating disorder called anorexia. Individuals with anorexia might view themselves as obese even though they are actually seriously underweight. They might severely restrict how much they eat, avoid certain foods they think are bad for them, exercise too much, and routinely put their bodies into starvation mode. Anorexia is very harmful—it can lead to heart, kidney, and breathing problems; broken bones; and confusion. People with eating disorders usually need professional help to overcome their issues with weight and food.

Eighteen-year-old Zoe Prather of Lawrence, Kansas, has undergone treatment for anorexia several times. She traces her food issues to being unhappy with her appearance and the high she experienced when people complimented her when she lost weight. She says, "I've kind of always felt like I don't belong and I shouldn't be here, and I'll never be pretty enough or skinny enough and once you start losing weight and feel like you have control over something, it's hard to stop."

Prather adds, "I want to get to a place in my life where maybe I don't love my home [body], and I didn't get to pick it, but to be content with it and . . . continue to keep it healthy and clean—and living."

Quoted in Mackenzie Clark, "Healthy Outlook: Silencing 'the Voice'—Lawrence Teen Shares Her Battle with Anorexia," *Lawrence (KS) Journal-World*, March 4, 2018. www2.ljworld.com.

comments about your own weight. Ideally, it would be great for parents to resolve their own body image issues, but this can be more challenging. This is not to say that we should never talk about weight, but rather to do so minimally and only within the context of health."[45]

Early Intervention Is Key

Parents of obese children would do well to intervene early because it is much easier for young children to lose weight than it is for teenagers or adults. Parents need to intervene because physicians are not always willing to point out a patient's weight problem since it may lead to an uncomfortable discussion. In addition, as medical school students, doctors do not receive much training in nutrition.

Another obstacle that can stand in the way of treating obese young people are rules health insurance companies set that affect which services they are willing to cover. Even though obesity is now considered a disease by the AMA, many health insurance companies do not recognize it as one. The result is that insurance companies will not cover the costs of treatment of obesity unless obesity has led to other ills, such as high blood pressure or fatty liver disease. Thus, parents may have to pay medical bills of thousands of dollars in order for their sons and daughters to receive treatment for obesity.

Caprigno says more medical professionals need to recognize that obesity is a disease and that obese patients need treatment just like individuals with other diseases. She says, "We definitely need to recognize that there's no one to blame for this and that there are genetic components that play a part, lifestyle plays a part, and we just need to change how we view obesity because there's such a stigma. We try to get everyone to understand that this is a disease. It's not something we choose."[46]

It many cases, it takes the assistance of parents as well as physicians and other professionals to help young patients develop new eating and lifestyle habits. Oftentimes, this type of teamwork can help young patients lose weight and keep it from coming back.

Chapter 5

Can Obesity Be Prevented?

Obesity in young people is a worldwide problem that will likely impact future generations for years to come. Turning the epidemic around will take a concerted effort on the part of governments, communities, schools, corporations, media, health care professionals, parents, and the patients themselves. The greatest impact will be achieved by doing everything possible to ensure that young people do not become overweight or obese, especially before they enter kindergarten.

Says New York City pediatrician Alvin N. Eden, "What has become increasingly obvious to me is that the only way to make any inroads into the problem of childhood obesity is to not let it happen in the first place. In other words, prevention—rather than treatment—is the key to success. The earlier you start, the better chance you have of preventing obesity from ever becoming a problem."[47]

However, while experts agree that steps should be taken, there is not yet consensus—or scientific proof—about what those steps should be. Yet there are many approaches being tried and some promising leads on how to prevent young people from becoming obese.

The Role of Schools

One place that can play a role in preventing obesity among young people is school. After all, since young people spend most of their time in school, it seems logical that schools could have a substantial role in reducing childhood obesity. Moreover, school is where students eat lunch five days a week. And school can also be the place where students could learn about nutrition, sports, and exercise. David Katz, creator of ABC for Fitness, a fitness program that can be incorporated into classrooms, explains that schools are important for preventing obesity. He says, "We take normally rambunctious children, send them to school, bolt them to chairs all day long so they can grow up to become adults who can't get off couches without crowbars."[48]

> "We take normally rambunctious children, send them to school, bolt them to chairs all day long so they can grow up to become adults who can't get off couches without crowbars."[48]
>
> —David Katz, creator of ABC for Fitness

Under ABC for Fitness, teachers build fitness into their daily lesson plans as part of what they teach. Children benefit from three- to five-minute intervals of physical activities interspersed throughout the day. For example, during a math lesson a teacher might have students stand up at their desk and participate in stretches, calisthenics, and a cooldown the teacher found in a free manual provided by the organization.

One study of one thousand students concluded that children who participated in the ABC for Fitness program had improved attention spans and better fitness scores than children who did not participate in the program.

Guidelines for What Students Eat

In addition to helping students become physically active, the CDC believes schools also have another role: helping them make smart choices in their diets. The CDC has proposed nine guidelines it would like schools to implement to encourage healthier eating as well as more physical activity among students. Among the nine strategies is providing meals with appealing foods that emphasize fruits, vegetables, and whole grains while also limiting students' exposure to salt, sugar, and cholesterol. In addition the CDC says schools should also present healthful choices in vending machines as well as snacks offered during classroom activities, fund-raisers, and after-school programs.

At least for younger students, those guidelines would also have to be followed by parents who often send snacks to school for the whole class to enjoy. Therefore, parents would be asked to provide only healthful snacks, avoiding cupcakes, candy, and sugary drinks, such as sodas.

The nation's premier health agency, the CDC, urges schools to offer healthful food to students who buy their meals. The agency guidelines stress adding more fruits, vegetables, and whole grains and limiting the amount of sugar, salt, and cholesterol.

Another guideline proposed by the CDC is creating a school environment in which physical activity and healthful eating are prioritized. In such an environment, weight-based teasing—including teasing by gym teachers—would not be tolerated. To promote physical activity, the CDC recommends schools provide students with an hour of physical activity each day through gym class as well as during recess and classroom activities.

Working with Communities

The CDC also suggests that schools work with surrounding communities to harness opportunities they present for nurturing health-

Negative Depictions in Kids' Movies

Children's movies are more than just a source of entertainment for children and parents. They may also carry subtle and not-so-subtle messages about what people eat and depict some characters as obese and not very bright.

To find out what messages children's movies are sending to young people, in 2017 a study at Duke University in North Carolina examined thirty-one PG- and G-rated movies that came out from 2012 through August 2015. They polled one hundred youths between the ages of nine and eleven to ask them which movies they had seen. Then they assigned raters to watch those movies to look for instances in which unhealthful foods were portrayed, people were seen eating in front of the television, or obese people were portrayed in negative ways. Such instances were found in every one of the thirty-one movies that were the subject of the study.

For instance, *The SpongeBob Movie*, based on the popular television cartoon by the same name, contains several troubling references. SpongeBob's best friend, Patrick, is portrayed as an overweight, dim-witted, and lazy starfish. In addition, in one scene another fish eating a hamburger is so obese that he breaks the chair when he sits down. The study's authors write, "It is important for parents and pediatricians to be aware of the cultural milieu of children and to provide active and conscious messaging endorsing healthful behaviors with the adoption of good habits that can last a lifetime."

Quoted in Tim Newman, "Kids' Movies Promote Poor Diet and Stigmatize Obesity," *Medical News Today*, December 7, 2017. www.medicalnewstoday.com.

ier lifestyles in young people. One example of the community-based initiative to which the CDC report refers is the after-school program My Daughter's Kitchen, which has been operating for five years in urban schools in Philadelphia, Pennsylvania, as well as neighboring Camden, New Jersey. With the help of seventy volunteers working in thirty-five schools, My Daughter's Kitchen encourages fifth- and sixth-grade students to master simple cooking skills such as chopping, stirring, and dicing as they create healthful and affordable meals they can make at home.

The program is comprised of eight weekly sessions, ending with students showing off their newfound skills by cooking for their parents such dishes as healthful breakfast burritos and baked cornflake chicken. A 2018 study on the program's performance found nearly half of students who participated said they were now eating more fruits and vegetables while 73 percent said they could tell the difference between processed foods and whole, natural foods. Meanwhile, more than half of the children were using their newfound cooking skills at home. This was exactly what ten-year-old Janaiyah English of Camden, New Jersey, was hoping for when she signed up for My Daughter's Kitchen. She says, "When I am 11, I want to make breakfast and dinner for my family."[49]

Students who participate in the program come to realize that when they prepare their own meals, they pay more attention to what they are eating. Michael Pollan, a journalist who writes extensively on nutrition, says learning to cook may be the most important skill young people can possess for maintaining their health throughout their lives. He says, "People who cook eat a healthier diet without giving it a thought."[50]

Hide the Junk Food

While teaching young people how to prepare their own meals is one way to provide them with good nutritional habits, the American Academy of Pediatrics (AAP) has explored other ways to prevent obesity among the young. In a list of recommendations issued in 2015, the AAP advised parents to limit their children's access to junk food—sugary beverages as well as snacks low in nutrition, such as cakes and candies—to special celebrations and to remove these foods from the home once the celebrations are over.

The AAP suggested parents offer five daily servings of fruits and vegetables. Also, the recommendations suggested parents place healthful foods where they can be seen, and if there are unhealthful foods in the house, to make them harder to find by putting them out of sight or wrapping them in opaque packaging. Parents are also asked to engage with their children in active play for one hour every day, to remove television sets from children's bedrooms, and to limit kids' use of cell phones and tablets. By turning off the television and other devices, children will be avoiding commercials that tempt them to ask for junk foods and high-calorie beverages.

Taxing Sugary Beverages

While parents play an important role in setting the tone for family health, they do not bear that responsibility alone. Some people argue that city governments are also responsible for ensuring the health of residents. For example, some city governments have levied taxes on sugary drinks—sodas, energy drinks, and sports drinks—to not only discourage people from buying them but also to raise revenues that can be used to fund prekindergarten classes, community schools, and other initiatives that help underserved populations. These taxes have proved controversial.

In 2017 Philadelphia became the first big city in the nation to pass a sugary drinks tax, adding 1.5 cents per ounce (28 g) to the purchase price of sweet beverages. (The much smaller college town of Berkeley, California, had adopted a sweet beverage tax in 2014.) Other cities soon adopted similar levies, including San Francisco and Oakland (both in California); Boulder, Colorado; and the cities in Cook County, Illinois.

In an effort to discourage people from buying colas and other sugary drinks, some cities have added special taxes on the sale of these drinks. The money generated from these taxes is usually applied to schools and other public services.

In 2018 Seattle, Washington, joined them by adding its own 1.75 cents per ounce tax to most sweetened drinks. Seattle health professionals Nwando Anyaoku and Diane Oakes have defended the tax. Anyaoku, director of pediatrics for Swedish Health Services in Seattle, and Oakes, president of the Arcora Foundation, a nonprofit group promoting oral health care, write:

At 1.75 cent tax for each ounce of sugary beverage, or an additional 21 cents for a 12-ounce soda, might seem like a lot at first. But the human and financial toll of not doing anything is even higher. Advertisers relentlessly promote sugary drinks to low-income households and communities of color. In the end, these vulnerable populations pay the price for our society's ready access to beverages that hold no nutritional value. So, it makes sense to direct revenue from the new tax to reduce health disparities where they are most predominant.[51]

The taxes in Philadelphia and other cities have run into opposition from the American Beverage Association, a trade group that represents businesses that deliver and sell beverages. These businesses are concerned the taxes will result in loss of profits under the assumption that if the price of a can of soda goes up, fewer people would be inclined to buy soda. In Seattle, a committee calling itself Yes! To Affordable Groceries worries that other cities in Washington State would adopt similar taxes. The group has suggested that cities would eventually add taxes to other foods as well. "Pro-tax advocates are pushing for special taxes on basic foods they dislike, such as meat,"[52] the group alleges.

Seattle's beverage tax is expected to raise $15 million a year while Philadelphia raised nearly $80 million during the first year it collected the tax. Philadelphia devoted the revenue from the tax to establishing educational programs for some 5,500 prekindergarten students. Revenue from the tax was also used to improve parks, libraries, and recreation centers. Says Philadelphia finance director Rob Dubow, "Thousands of children are getting access to pre-K and to community schools that they would not have gotten without this tax. So from our perspective, it's a big success."[53]

> "Thousands of children are getting access to pre-K and to community schools that they would not have gotten without this [sugary beverage] tax. So from our perspective, it's a big success."[53]
>
> —Philadelphia finance director Rob Dubow

Rethinking Sodas and Snacks

While the sugary drinks tax in Philadelphia and other cities has helped establish programs for very young students, there is also no question that the fears of the beverage drink industry have been realized: Whether they live in cities that impose such taxes, or simply are more mindful of their own nutrition, it is clear that sugary drinks are less popular than in years past. A 2016 report by the British research group Mintel Group Ltd. revealed that some 25 percent of Americans admitted to ordering fewer sodas when they dine out compared to the year before. While such a statistic may

Lessons from School Lunches in Japan

The Japanese do not have a big problem with childhood obesity. One reason is that school lunches, starting in elementary school, come with an education on healthy eating. Beginning in elementary school, students learn about what is in their food. They eat together in their classrooms—after they have served the lunch to their classmates while wearing white hats and spotless smocks. Says Masahiro Oji, government director of school health education in Japan, "Japan's standpoint is that school lunches are a part of education, not a break from it."

Everyone eats the same lunch that was made that morning using fresh locally sourced ingredients. Elementary school and middle school students are not allowed to bring their lunches from home. Lunch usually consists of a combination of soup, rice, and vegetables. The low-cost food ingredients are paid for by parents although subsidies are available for families that cannot afford to pay.

School lunches are good enough that parents are sometimes envious. "Parents hear their kids talking about what they had for lunch and kids ask them to re-create the meals at home," says Tatsuji Shino, an elementary school principal in Tokyo.

By the time teens are in high school, they are free to bring what they like for lunch but have likely absorbed what they need to know to make healthy selections.

Quoted in Chris Weller, "Japan's Mouthwatering School Lunch Program Is a Model for the Rest of the World," *Business Insider*, March 27, 2017. www.businessinsider.com.

cause concern among many executives in the beverage industry, other executives realize that accommodating changing consumer tastes and trends is a part of being in business.

PepsiCo, the company that produces the very familiar soft drink Pepsi, as well as numerous other food and beverage products, has looked into the future and has decided that to meet consumers' needs, it will make its products more healthful. Among the company's other familiar products are Mountain Dew and 7UP beverages as well as Frito-Lay, Ruffles, and Cheetos snack foods.

PepsiCo has announced that by 2025, it will lower the amount of sugar and salt in its products. Indra Nooyi, the company's CEO, says, "To meet the evolving needs of our consumers around the world, we are shifting our portfolio to a wider range of what we call . . . 'everyday nutrition products,' which are products with positive nutrients like grains, fruits and vegetables or protein."[54]

The strategy seems to be paying off as the company is already earning nearly half of its revenues from its more healthful new products. They include potato chips that are baked instead of fried and a version of 7UP with 30 percent less sugar. In addition, PepsiCo has introduced LIFEWTR, a bottled water product with no added sugar and, therefore, zero calories. Says Brad Jakeman, president of PepsiCo's Global Beverage Group, "We are starting to see water play a greater role in the repertoire of a consumer's beverage consumption. I think we are seeing a secular and irreversible trend toward healthier beverages."[55]

> "We are shifting our portfolio to a wider range of what we call . . . 'everyday nutrition products,' which are products with positive nutrients like grains, fruits and vegetables or protein."[54]
>
> —Indra Nooyi, CEO of Pepsico

Childhood Obesity and Politics

While corporations like PepsiCo make many of their decisions based on their financial outlook, the federal government is ca-

First Lady Michelle Obama works with a young invited guest in the White House Kitchen Garden. While her husband was in office, the two promoted youth fitness and healthful eating through their Let's Move program.

pable of making decisions based on what is best for the public. In the past the desire to prevent obesity in young children has reached as high as the president and First Lady. During the presidency of Barack Obama, from 2009 through early 2017, First Lady Michelle Obama made childhood fitness and nutrition her top priority. To embody the change she hoped to create throughout the nation, she created a White House vegetable garden and invited neighborhood children to tend it.

Moreover, President Obama assembled the first national task force on childhood obesity. Its mission was to find ways to create healthier American families. The Obamas called their fitness program Let's Move. In addition to signaling that childhood obesity deserved to be a national priority, Let's Move accomplished other goals. For example, during the Obama administration

Congress adopted the 2010 Healthy, Hunger-Free Kids Act, which updated fifteen-year-old nutritional standards and provided the first increase in federal spending in thirty years, enabling American schools to provide more healthful lunches and snacks for 50 million children.

Let's Move also supported establishing more salad bars in school cafeterias. As its name implies, Let's Move encouraged children to exercise for sixty minutes a day and promoted the idea that young people and families should spend more time in the nation's parklands. Under the Every Kid in a Park plan, fourth-grade students and their families can obtain free admission passes for a year to some two thousand US parks and waterways. Walking in public parks is a good way for families to exercise together in a beautiful setting and step away from their cell phones, computer games, and TVs.

Following the departure of the Obamas, the administration of President Donald Trump has been less inclined to pursue nutritional programs in schools as well as other antiobesity efforts. The White House Office of Management and Budget, which helps decide how federal dollars are spent, has questioned the need to spend tax dollars on antiobesity programs. As reported via the online magazine *Business Insider*, "Considering that 20 percent of kids eat breakfast at school and more than 90 percent get lunch there, the grains and sugar preferences they develop in the cafeteria likely shape the nutrition choices they'll make later in life."[56]

Roles for Children and Teens

Just as corporations, politicians, schools, and parents have roles in preventing teens and children from becoming obese, there are also places for young people in the antiobesity fight. In addition to drinking fewer sodas and fruit juices, eating more nutritious meals at home with their parents, and devoting more time to sports and exercise, young people might think about putting themselves in the shoes of their overweight classmates. Realizing how lonely some of these peers may be and what health struggles they might be coping with could lead to more empathy and fewer fat jokes and unkind comments. Young people whose weight makes them the subject of teasing tend to put on more weight. "Overweight kids who experience peer rejection and social isolation are likely to exercise less, have greater food intake and have fewer positive role models for healthy habits and a healthy weight,"[57] says Kayla de La Haye, professor of medicine at the University of Southern California in Los Angeles.

In addition, experts agree that while the obesity epidemic did not occur overnight, the solutions to it are likely to emerge gradually. Write Jacob C. Warren and K. Bryant Smalley,

> The fight against childhood obesity will be epic—we have never before faced a threat to the health of our nation that directly impacts so many people; the majority of Americans, in fact. Change will require persistence, drive and tough decision-making. It will take years to turn the tide, and many people coming together to change our nation. Our children cannot lead this charge themselves—we must take it on for them. This change will require all of us. But after all, aren't our children worth it?[58]

Clearly, preventing obesity is a long-term goal that benefits both society and individuals. It is by no means an easy task and more research needs to be done on the best possible methods for achieving that goal. But if the challenge is great so too are the rewards.

Source Notes

Introduction: A Global Crisis

1. Quoted in Teens Bulletin Board, Blubber Buster, August 18, 2017. www.blubberbuster.com.
2. Quoted in Andrew Pollack, "A.M.A. Recognizes Obesity as a Disease," *New York Times*, June 18, 2013. www.nytimes.com.
3. Quoted in Harvard T.H. Chan School of Public Health, "More than Half of US Children Will Have Obesity as Adults If Certain Trends Continue," November 29, 2017. www.hsph.harvard.edu.
4. Jacob C. Warren and K. Bryant Smalley, *Always the Fat Kid*. New York: Palgrave Macmillan, 2013, p. 179.
5. Julia Belluz, "White House Officials Think Childhood Obesity Is Not a Problem," Vox.com, October 20, 2017. www.vox.com.

Chapter 1: What Is Obesity?

6. Carl J. Lavie, *The Obesity Paradox*. New York: Hudson Street, 2014, p. 3.
7. Anonymous, "I'm Morbidly Obese," Experience Project, August 12, 2011. www.experienceproject.com/stories/Am-Morbidly-Obese/1718783.
8. Christian Nordqvist, "Why BMI Is Inaccurate and Misleading," *Medical News Today*, August 25, 2013. www.medicalnewstoday.com.
9. Warren and Smalley, *Always the Fat Kid*, p. 18.
10. Edward Abramson, "Is Your Child Overweight or Is It Just Baby Fat?," *Psychology Today*, December 18, 2010. www.psychologytoday.com.
11. Quoted in Sarah Frostenson, "More American Children and Teens Aren't Just Obese. They're Morbidly Obese," Vox.com, April 26, 2016. www.vox.com.

12. Quoted in Frostenson, "More American Children and Teens Aren't Just Obese."

13. Sara Chodosh, "Fat but Fit Is Absolutely Possible," *Popular Science*, May 29, 2017. www.popsci.com.

14. Quoted in Marcia Frellick, "AMA Declares Obesity a Disease," *Medscape Medical News*, June 19, 2013. www.medscape.com.

15. Quoted in Rosie Taylor, "How 'Fit but Fat' Is a Myth," *Daily Mail* (London), August 15, 2017. www.dailymail.co.uk.

Chapter 2: What Causes Obesity?

16. Sujit Sharma, "Are Fast Food Ads Killing Us?," CNN, April 27, 2017. www.cnn.com.

17. Richard Alleyne, "Athletes Burn More Energy Even When Resting, Researchers Claim," *Telegraph* (London), October 20, 2008. www.telegraph.co.uk.

18. Peter A. Ubel, "Chew on This: Willpower Predicts How Quickly You Taste Food," *Psychology Today*, February 19, 2008. www.psychologytoday.com.

19. Quoted in Julie Beck, "You Can't Willpower Your Way to Lasting Weight Loss," *Atlantic*, June 25, 2016. www.theatlantic.com.

20. Joy Manning, "5 Surprising Facts About Willpower," WebMD, July 29, 2014. www.webmd.com.

21. S.A. Leonard et al., "Weight Gain in Pregnancy and Child Weight Status from Birth to Adulthood in the United States," *Pediatric Obesity*, June 28, 2016. www.ncbi.nlm.nih.gov.

22. Sharma, "Are Fast Food Ads Killing Us?"

23. Eric Schlosser, *Fast Food Nation*. New York: Mariner Books, 2012, p. 4.

24. Quoted in Greg McFarlane, "'Healthifying' the Fast Food Market," Investopedia, 2018. www.investopedia.com.

25. Quoted in Alice Park, "Teens Are Just as Sedentary as 60-Year-Olds," *Time*, June 16, 2017. http://time.com.

Chapter 3: What Is It Like to Live with Obesity?

26. Quoted in Jacque Wilson, "Why Is It So Hard for Kids to Lose Weight?," CNN, February 16, 2012. www.cnn.com.

27. Quoted in Harriet Brown, "Feeling Bullied by Parents About Weight," *Well* (blog), *New York Times*, January 9, 2013. https://well.blogs.nytimes.com.
28. Anonymous, "I'm Morbidly Obese."
29. Quoted in Annalisa Barbieri, "I'm 13 and Worried About Being Fat," *Guardian* (Manchester, UK), January 20, 2017. www.theguardian.com.
30. Nicolas Stettler, with Susan Shelly, *Living with Obesity*. New York: Facts On File, 2009, p. 51.
31. Quoted in Recovery.org, "Morbidly Obese and Depressed," March 2016. www.recovery.org.
32. Quoted in Shamard Charles, "High Blood Pressure Diagnoses Could Increase Among Teens, Kids," NBC News, August 21, 2017. www.nbcnews.com.
33. Quoted in CBS News, "How Can We Slow the Alarming Rise of Type 2 Diabetes in Children?," November 17, 2017. www.cbsnews.com.
34. Quoted in Nicolette Schleisman, "Love Your Heart: Pediatric Heart Health," KSLA, February 8, 2018. www.ksla.com.
35. Quoted in Anahad O'Connor, "Threat Grows from Liver Illness Tied to Obesity," *Well* (blog), *New York Times*, June 13, 2014. https://well.blogs.nytimes.com.
36. Robert H. Lustig, *Fat Chance: Beating the Odds Against Sugar, Processed Food, Obesity, and Disease.* New York: Hudson Street, 2013, pp. 150–51.

Chapter 4: Can Obesity Be Treated?

37. Quoted in Elizabeth Landau, "Teen Who Lost 100 Pounds: I Did It, and You Can Too," CNN, October 21, 2013. www.cnn.com.
38. Jennifer Kraschnewski, "Why Your Doctor Can't Help You Lose Weight," *Philadelphia Inquirer*, December 31, 2017, p. G4.
39. Quoted in Wilson, "Why Is It So Hard for Kids to Lose Weight?"
40. Rachel DeHaven, "How One Health Professional Addresses the Stigma Around Childhood Obesity," *Philadelphia Inquirer*, November 30, 2017. www.philly.com.
41. Quoted in Warren and Smalley, *Always the Fat Kid*, p. 80.
42. Quoted in Warren and Smalley, *Always the Fat Kid*, p. 187.
43. Quoted in Kelly Wallace, "2-Year-Old Gets Weight-Loss Surgery: How Young Is Too Young?," CNN, September 21, 2013. www.cnn.com.

44. Quoted in Wallace, "2-Year-Old Gets Weight-Loss Surgery."

45. Quoted in Anna Almendrala, "This Is the Worst Way to Talk to Your Children About Weight," *Huffington Post*, June 27, 2016. www.huffingtonpost.com.

46. Quoted in Wallace, "2-Year-Old Gets Weight-Loss Surgery."

Chapter 5: Can Obesity Be Prevented?

47. Alvin N. Eden, "Obesity Prevention in Children," *Pediatrics for Parents*, March 8, 2018. https://pedsforparents.com.

48. Quoted in Mika Brezezinski, *Obsessed*. New York: Weinstein Books, 2013, p. 189.

49. Quoted in Maureen Fitzgerald, "Lessons That Go Beyond the Kitchen," *Philadelphia Inquirer*, March 8, 2018, p. D1.

50. Quoted in Fitzgerald, "Lessons That Go Beyond the Kitchen."

51. Nwando Anyaoku and Diane Oakes, "21 Extra Cents for That Soda? It's Worth It," Crosscut, March 7, 2018. https://crosscut.com.

52. Quoted in Daniel Beckman, "Beverage Industry, Allies Start Campaign to Stop Seattle's Soda Tax from Spreading," *Seattle Times*, February 28, 2018. www.seattletimes.com.

53. Quoted in Laura McCrystal, "Philly Soda Tax Revenue Falling Short, City Adjusts Plans for Pre-K and Other Programs," *Philadelphia Inquirer*, March 1, 2018. www.philly.com.

54. Quoted in Lauren Thomas, "Pepsi Doubles Down on 'Guilt-Free' Options in Effort to Boost Sales," CNBC.com, April 26, 2017. www.cnbc.com.

55. Quoted in John Kell, "PepsiCo to Launch Premium Water Brand LIFEWTR," *Fortune*, December 9, 2016. wwwfortune.com.

56. Hilary Brueck, "Kids Are Eating Less Whole Grains and More Sugary Milk in School Lunches This Year—See How Federal Rules Have Changed for the Worse," *Business Insider*, January 11, 2018. www.businessinsider.com.

57. Quoted in Jacqueline Howard, "The Children Most Likely to Be Bullied by Their Own Friends," CNN, July 7, 2017. www.cnn.com.

58. Warren and Smalley, *Always the Fat Kid*, p. 190.

Organizations and Websites

American Academy of Pediatrics (AAP)

345 Park Blvd.
Itasca, IL 60143
website: www.aap.org

The AAP is a professional organization composed of sixty-six thousand primary care pediatricians and related specialists dedicated to the health of infants, children, and adolescents. Its website contains numerous articles on weight, including studies, weight gain in football, and weight bias.

American Dietetic Association

120 S. Riverside Plaza, Suite 2000
Chicago, IL 60606-6995
websites: www.diet.com and www.eatright.org

The American Dietetic Association is the largest association of food and nutrition professionals with more than sixty-seven thousand members dedicated to fostering healthy lifestyles. Visitors to the association's websites can find meal plans by calories, recipes for healthy snacks and foods, and blog entries on nutrition topics.

Center for Science in the Public Interest

220 L St. NW, Suite 300
Washington, DC 20005
website: https://cspinet.org

The Center for Science in the Public Interest is an independent organization that offers science-based advice for maintaining a healthy diet and advocates for a healthy food system. The organization produces the *Nutrition Action Healthletter* and is a proponent of keeping junk food out of schools, reducing soda consumption, and making food labeling more transparent.

National Association to Advance Fat Acceptance (NAAFA)

PO Box 4662
Foster City, CA 94404-0662
website: www.naafaonline.com

NAAFA is an all-volunteer organization whose mission is to eliminate discrimination and raise awareness of the rights of fat children and adults. Its website offers a tool kit that can be used to advocate for fat children experiencing weight bias, as well as an outline of the issues faced by obese people. Its site also lists events the organization plans and policy recommendations for educational institutions.

National Eating Disorders Association

200 W. Forty-First St., Suite 1203
New York, NY 10036
website: www.nationaleatingdisorders.org

The group is the largest nonprofit organization serving 20 million women and 10 million men and their families who have eating disorders. Its website provides information on eating disorders, including warning signs, prevention, statistics, and treatment, as well as an accessible help line.

Rudd Center for Food Policy and Obesity

University of Connecticut
One Constitution Plaza, Suite 600
Hartford, CT 06103
website: www.uconnruddcenter.org

The Rudd Center for Food Policy and Obesity promotes solutions to childhood obesity, poor diet, and weight bias through research and policy. The organization's website features videos of teens talking about weight bias. The site also provides links to news stories that deal with childhood obesity, such as fighting obesity in preschool students.

US Centers for Disease Control and Prevention (CDC)

600 Clifton Rd.
Atlanta, GA 30329-4027
website: www.cdc.gov

The CDC is a federal agency charged with protecting Americans from threats to their health, safety, and security. The agency's website has many pages devoted to obesity issues and includes an online calculator to determine body mass index.

For Further Research

Books

Laura Dawes, *Childhood Obesity in America: Biography of an Epidemic*. Cambridge, MA: Harvard University Press, 2014.

Alvin N. Eden, Barbara J. Moore, and Adrienne Forman, *Fit from the Start: How to Prevent Childhood Obesity in Infancy*. Clyde Park, MT: Shape Up America, 2014.

Michelle P. Maidenberg, *Free Your Child from Overeating: A Handbook for Helping Kids and Teens*. New York: The Experiment, 2016.

Andrea C. Nakaya, *Thinking Critically: Obesity.* San Diego, CA: ReferencePoint, 2018.

Kristin Voigt, Stuart G. Nicholls, and Garrath Williams, *Childhood Obesity: Ethical and Policy Issues*. New York: Oxford University Press, 2014.

Internet Sources

Annalisa Barbieri, "I'm 13 and Worried About Being Fat," *Guardian* (Manchester, UK), January 20, 2017. www.theguardian.com /lifeandstyle/2017/jan/20/im-13-and-worried-about-being-fat.

Sarah Frostenson, "More American Children and Teens Aren't Just Obese. They're Morbidly Obese," Vox.com, April 26, 2016. www.vox.com/2016/4/26/11490206/children-teens-morbidly -obese.

Meghan Holohan, "The 5 Steps This Teen Took to Lose 142 Pounds in 2 Years and Transform Her Life," Today.com, July 5, 2017.

www.today.com/health/teen-loses-143-pounds-2-years-trans
forms-life-t113369.

Marc Michalsky, "Weight-Loss Surgery for Kids: A Good Idea,
Despite Many Misconceptions," *U.S. News & World Report*,
June 18, 2015. https://health.usnews.com/health-news/blogs
/eat-run/2015/06/18/weight-loss-surgery-for-kids-a-good-idea
-despite-many-misconceptions.

Andrew Pollack, "A.M.A. Recognizes Obesity as a Disease," *New
York Times*, June 18, 2013. www.nytimes.com/2013/06/19/busi
ness/ama-recognizes-obesity-as-a-disease.html.

Index

Note: Boldface page numbers indicate illustrations.